HOW TO

MY KINDLE LIBRARY/DEVICE

A complete step by step guide to manage

your kindle library: add books, gift,

achieve, delete, lend, share, return books

and manage family library (tips and

tricks)

BY

APRIL SMITH

TABLE OF CONTENT

Introduction

Owning a Kindle Fire tablet is fine. But being able to manage the content on your Kindle library or device is just great. A lot of new users of the Kindle device have expressed how difficult it was for them trying to understand the whole Kindle library stuffs the first time.

This book was written to help users seamlessly savor and manage their Kindle library. Topics covered include, but not limited to, downloading cloud contents, transferring contents from an old device to a new one, purchasing boos as gifts, borrowing kindle books, archiving used kindle books, and finally creating, sharing and deleting contents from your kindle library.

The last part of this book culminates with practical solutions to common problems that can affect your Kindle Fire tablet.

The best thing about this book is its simplicity and practicability. Haven written many titles on topics relating to the Kindle fire tablet, the author proves his experience and understanding of everything Kindle; from the kindle device to the kindle library. This user guide is at its best.

Kindly read on.

Chapter One

How to Manage Content on Kindle Library or Device

How to sort Kindle content

In the course of using your Kindle device, of course you'll load it up with books. And after loading up it can get kind of messy. Yeah sure you can just delete the books you don't need again but sometimes some books are just too dear to our heart that we can't bear to see them go. But they are still making a mess of your library.

In situations like this, all you have to do is sort them. And sorting with the Kindle can be said to be simple. One of the most recommended ways to sort is through the **List view** option.

1. At the upper part of your library, you should see option for **All Items**

2. Choose **List view**

3. You should find the sorting menu just beside **All Items**. Select it

4. You'll be shown different options to sort your books. Choose the one you desire.

- With **Recent**, your books will appear in the same order that you opened them previously. The book you were reading last will be shown at the top of the list. Not a bad option you could say.

- **Author** and **Title** quite explains itself. According to the criteria, it will sort them alphabetically.

- **Collections** can also be said to be folders. Collections will appear at the top of the list. If there's a book you've not put to collection, it will appear under the collections. You can use this method to fix a certain book at the top.

If you chose the **Recent** method or the **Author** and **Title**, the books that you fix in Collection will still appear in the main library. It doesn't matter how many collections you create, these or methods to sort will still triumph and show up in the other books you have.

How to Download cloud contents

You have the ability to sync your Kindle with other devices and receive contents wirelessly. These contents have been sent to the **Manage your Content and Devices** option on the website. Once you've linked your contents through all of your devices, you can then download content that's has been uploaded or even updates.

If you purchase any Digital content from the Amazon website, it will be kept in the Cloud content library. This content library is for you to access and download then contents. But before you can start to download anything, you need to ensure that you've connected your Kindle wirelessly. Once you've done that, then we can sync all the contents

To synchronize all the contents,

1. Swipe downwards from the top of the display.

2. After the Quick settings have been revealed, select **Sync**.

If you want to sync to the latest page you last read on you Kindle deice,

1. Open up the book and go to the page you stopped

2. And as you read the book, touch the screen at the center.

3. Choose the option titled, **Sync to the furthest Page Read**

Now to download content from the cloud

1. Go to the home of your device and select a Kindle content library. You can select Books

2. You should see the tab for **Cloud**. If you tap it, you'll be able to see

the content that you've purchased
but are not downloaded to your
device

3. To download it to your device,
   select the content you wish to get.

4. To see you content, to the tab for
   Devices.

1. This is good option to get books on your Kindle as you don't need to be connected to the internet on your Kindle. But first you want to download the book to your computer. If you have an ebook that you want to transfer to your Kindle,

   - Sign in to your Amazon account

   - Choose **Account & Lists**

   - Then **Your Content and Devices**

- Select the **menu icon** at the left of the book

- Select **Download & transfer via USB**

- Choose your device

2. Convert the Kindle. If the ebook that you downloaded is not in PDF, AZW or MOBI, you'll have to convert it.

3. Plug the USB cable to your computer and the other end to your Kindle like you want charge it.

- If you use a Mac and you don't have ports for USB, you can get a USB adapter for the computer to be able to transfer

4. Open up the your Kindle device In the computer

- With Mac, you'll have to open **Finder** and choose your Kindle from the left side

- With Windows, enter the **File Explorer** and then **This PC**. Click your Kindle twice to open it up

5. From your computer, Open up the documents folder in your Kindle

   - If you don't see the documents folder, then you have to click and open the **Internal storage**

   - With Kindle fire you might want to open up the folder for **Books**

6. Copy the file you downloaded and converted and paste in the document folder.

   - To copy you can just press Ctrl+C and paste with Ctrl+V for Windows

- To copy and paste on a Mac, use Command+C and Command+V

- You have to wait for a while for the ebook to finish transferring. Once the book has been transferred, you can then eject the cable from your computer and your Kindle

How to transfer content from your old device to a new one

Okay you just got your new Kindle. But you miss the books you got on your old Kindle device. You wish you would go through those interesting books again. It would make no sense to purchase them again. Why would you, you can still get them from Amazon.

Just transfer, that way you don't get to miss any content. You will be able to move the books or contents to your new device with your computer.

1. Hold on. Before you grab your PC. Take your new Kindle and log In with the same account you used with your old device. This way you'll be able to use the same account to move content

2. Now you can get your computer. Enter the Amazon website in your computer's browser by going to www.amazon.com. If your not signed, hit the **Sign in** button

3. Move your cursor to your name right above **Account & List** at the menu bar.

4. Select your content and devices

5. Your content and books should show up now. Tick the box beside each book that you would want to move.

6. Click **Deliver**. You should find the Deliver button right next to the **Delete** button above all your book list.

7. Hit the option **Devices Selected** and select the Kindle you want to transfer it to (your new Kindle)

8. Now at the bottom right of the window, you should see another **Deliver** button. Click it. With this, all the books and content that you selected, will be transferred and moved over to your new Kindle or the Kindle that you selected

Chapter Two

How to Purchase Kindle Books as Gifts

You may be already planning on surprising someone with an eBook as a gift. Good thinking! EBooks can be said to be the ideal gift to give that loved one. It can be because of your daughter's graduation, of you want to show your friend how much your care, books can make a perfect present.

Gifting eBooks is like the easiest thing to do. Know why? You really don't need to leave your home. You don't have to ride all around town going through stores. You can just relax on your couch send your wonderful package.

There's no specific gift you can give. You can do something as low as $4 or as high as 60 bucks for months unlimited Kindle membership. If you're thinking that you can just go out and buy a printed book, wrap it and send it, you might want to think again. Because you see, not all books actually get printed.

There are some brilliant books from different genres like fantasy or romance that never gets the chance of living on real paper, only digitally. So if you're thinking only of physical books, you might be missing out on a whole lot of fun and literary adventure. In fact not only you, the people you're giving a gift too.

You have the ability to gift someone a Kindle book that is available in the Kindle store as long as you've got their email address. Yep, that's what you'll be using. And even if you don't have an Amazon device, you can still show some love and gift Kindle books.

But as long as the person you're giving has a valid email address and a Kindle app or Kindle device, then you're good to go. But first, you want to validate your 1-Click payment method in your account.

1. Move over to **Manage Your Content and Devices**

2. Under the **Settings** tab, select **Edit Payment Method**

Now to purchase a Kindle book as a gift,

1. Enter the Amazon website and sign in to your account

2. Move over to the Kindle store and choose the book you wish to gift. But note that Amazon says that you can't gift books on pre order and free books for now.

3. After you're taken to the page that shows the details of the book, select the button that says **Buy for others**

4. Input the email address of the person you want to give the book as a gift to. Enter the other information required.

5. You can put the date of delivery and a gift message. But you can skip the message part if you don't want to. But really you should add something.

6. Select **Place your order** to complete purchase.

You also have the option to redeliver a book if you've already purchased. To do this

1. Go to **Your Account**

2. Then select **Your Digital Orders**

3. Choose the button for **Resend E-mail**, this should be in the page for Order Summary

How to borrow and lend Kindle books to a friend

Now we are all about sharing. Because when many read books, what they really love to do is share them and talk about them with both family and friends. Of course buying a book from the store, reading and going through the adventures packed in it can be most thrilling. But it can be kind of awkward telling your friends about this awesome book and how you enjoyed then they ask you to show them but you say 'Oh no you have to buy it.'

Spread the love around and just share it. Yes, Amazon makes it possible for you to share some books to your friends, family or virtually anybody you wish. But you need to have the email address that it connected with their account on Amazon.

You can loan a book to someone in two ways you can do it from the product detail page or through the page for **Manage Your Content and Devices**

To lend a book through the product detail page,

1. Look for the book in Amazon. You can either search for the book from the homepage (easy way) or you can go through the Kindle store (long way but you also get to have a view of other interesting titles)

2. If the book you selected has already been purchased by you, you will be notified at the top. If a book is available to be lent, you will see the option **Loan this**

book. If you don't see it, then you cannot lend this book

3. After you've selected **Loan this book**, you'll be asked to input the email address of the person you want to loan. Put in the email and **Send now**.

4. The book will be sent the person's email and they'll be able to download it to their device

To lend through **Manage Your Content and Devices**

1. Enter the **Manage Your Content and Devices** page

2. After you've found the book you want to lend, select the menu icon right beside the title.

3. If this book is available to be lent, you'll see the **Loan this title** option. If you don't see it, then you could say that the book cannot be lent

4. After selecting this Loan this title, you'll be asked to input the information of the person you want to lend the book to. Like the

email address, the other information is said to be optional.

5. Hit **Send now** and a link will be sent to their email for them to download the book.

How to get gift cards

You can get Kindle gift cards from a number of places but if you want a large choice of card designs and delivery options, you definitely want to go through the Amazon.com route. Amazon gives you a wide option for you for buy Kindle gift cards. It can be done through online delivery via Facebook, email or even in PDF.

As with Kindle gift card, they don't have an expiration date so this means that they are well valid till the receiver uses them.

The 'No expiration date' option is not really need as readers don't take much time before they grab the opportunity to read

You can include a message to say congratulations or something like that and they will be sent to the recipients inbox or you can even state that it should be sent to their Facebook

You can get Gift cards in advance so that the date doesn't skip your mind and the recipient will get it at the specified date.

You can get a gift card by logging in and going to **Your Account** in your Amazon account

1. Connect your device to a Wi-Fi network. To do this swipe down from the top, switch on Wi-Fi and chose a network

2. Select **Books** tab from the home screen and find the books you wish to archive. You can also hit the search bar to find the book

3. Long press the book and two options should appear, choose the option **Remove from Device**.

   - Don't be afraid of removing from device, that's the whole

point of this. If you don't
remove from device, then
you're not archiving anything

- Even after you've selected
  Remove from device, it is still
  available in the Cloud, kept
  safe for you

4. In your home screen select books.
   At the top corners of the screen
   you will see **All** or **Cloud** and
   Device. Choose **All/Cloud**. This
   will show up the books that have
   been stored on the cloud

- Scroll to find the book that you want to put back your device. Tap it to download it again on your device. If there a book that is in your device already, you will find a checkmark right next to the title.

Chapter Three

How to Create a Family Library and Share Books with Family Members

After ages of waiting, the option of sharing books with your partner or children is now available to Kindle owners. This is possible through the family library. With this method you don't have to worry about buying books all the time, you just tell your family member share to it with you.

If you want to start to share books with the family library, the two adults set have to first authorize themselves for them to use the methods of payment connected to their accounts on Amazon. When the adults do this, it will not disturb the existing payment settings of the adult.

An adult can just easily copy the method of payment from the other adult's to their own account.

If you want to add an adult,

1. Go to the home screen and choose **Menu**

2. Hit **Settings**

3. Choose **Household & Family Library**. If you're using an older device, you might have to choose **Registration and Household** before selecting **household and family library**

4. Select the option to **Add a New Person**

5. Select **Add Adult**

6. Give your device to the adult you want to add. They will have to enter the email address associated with their Amazon account and then their password. The can

create a new account if they don't have an account already.

7. After they have entered their email and password, they will be able to share their content with you. They can be generous and share all the content they've purchased or they might take it easy and share just some titles

8. Then you'll now have the opportunity to enable the option for sharing

You also have the opportunity of adding a maximum of 4 child profiles and you can select the content that you can share with the children. To add a child,

1. Enter the home screen and select the **Menu**

2. Select **Settings**

3. Then **Household & Family Library**

4. Choose **Add a New Person**

5. Select **Add Child**

6. Input your password and then the information of the child (gender, name and other)

7. Choose the contents that you want add to the library of your child

8. Go through the profile and the reading settings of the child and hit **Done**

Before you can access the profiles that have been created from Amazon, you will need to connect your Kindle to a wireless network.

If you wish to leave household so you can stop sharing content, also to cancel the option of sharing payment methods,

1. Go to the home screen on your Kindle

2. Hit the **Menu** icon

3. Choose the **Settings**

4. If you're using older devices, you have to choose **Registration And Household** then select **Household & Family Library**. If using newer device, choose the **Household & Family Library** option instead

5. Choose the adult profile that wants to exit the household

6. And it you're prompted, Put in the password for the profile you selected

7. Press **Leave Household**

8. Hit **OK** to complete the process

Before you leave the household you want to think about it carefully. If you select the option to leave household, all the access to the contents and payment methods that were shared between the two adults will be lost. Also the adults will lose the prime benefits that was once shared from the second adult

If any of the adults goes away from the household, the two adults will not have the opportunity of entering the Amazon household with different adult. This 'ban' des not last forever, it's for 180 days. But that's a pretty hefty number of days.

But if you left the household by accident, you can move over to the **Manage Your Household** and you'll be able to join the same household with the same adult.

How to borrow books from a friend

If you happen to know someone else who has a Kindle. Could be a friend or family member, you have the opportunity to loan a book from them. This loaning does not last forever, of course Amazon said you could borrow not collect. So this only lasts for 14 days.

I know right, they should've made I something like 1 month. But If you're a fast reader and can complete before 14 days, you should have no problem. And in fact something you will find interesting is that the borrower doesn't even need a Kindle device. Those that have the app on their phones or computer can still access this feature.

But when borrowing you should remember that not all books are available for lending. And whether the book is available for lending, the fact that you'll get the book lies on the shoulder of the book owner. So make sure you fall on the good side of person because they have some work to do to lend

1. Direct the owner to go to www.amazon.com/mycd. They will have to navigate to book they want to borrow you.

2. Have them go **Manage your Content and Devices** in their own account

3. They will have to go to the **Action** box beside the title of the book and click it

4. They should see the option **Loan this Title**. If they happen not to see this option, then this book is

not available for lending. If they see it, they should click it.

5. From here, a form should show up now. Information will have to be filled like the name of lender and your email. After filing the necessary information that is required, they can click **Send Now**

6. Once they've sent the book, it will be available through the email. The title of the email should be something along the lines of **Get your Loaned Book Now**.

7. Now you'll have to sign in and choose a device to send the book that's been borrowed. After which you will select **Accept Loaned book**

There are many speedy readers who only take 3 days to finish a book. It's really not a hassle for them to complete the book in just 14 days. In fact the 14 days is way too convenient. If you're like that then you wouldn't want to wait till the 14 days are up before returning the book

Unfortunately, when many finish reading a book early, they try to find a way to return the book back to the owner but they don't find. It's a really simple task – just return the book. But they fumble around in the settings and go through the menu on their device and don't find the option to return.

And that's the main problem – searching for it in the device. You won't find it there. You have go through the Amazon website route

Retuning a loaned book is as easy as

1. Entering amazon.com in a browser on your computer

2. Logging in to your Amazon account

3. Going over to the **Manage Content and Devices** section

4. Hit the **Action** button that's beside the book you want to return

5. Select **Delete from Library**

6. To confirm that you want to return the book chose **Yes**

Chapter Four

How to Delete Kindle Books and Contents from Your Library

As you load your Kindle device with books, magazines or documents, the device can get kind of crowded. The best thing to do is just delete the content that you know you don't need any more and have become useless.

What's more, there is a method for you to delete your contents and items if it's not with you. This option is really useful if you lose your Kindle or it gets stolen.

Method one

Through the website

The website Is like the powerhouse of your Kindle. The instance that we just mentioned about if your device gets stolen can be solved with this method. You certainly don't want the thief to enjoy the content you took your time to install.

1. Enter the Amazon website and sign in to your account.

2. After signing in, you want to head over to the **Manage Your Content and Devices** segment. This will enable to go through the process to remove the content from your library

3. Head over to the tab that says **Your Content**. There's a big chance that when you sign in, the page that will be presented to you will not be the **Your Content** tab. So If you're somewhere else, you want to select **Your Content**

4. Now you'll be presented will a list of your books. These are the books you've purchased. You should see a column of boxes on the left of the title of the book you want to remove. Click it to tick the box of the book. If you would like to remove more than one book, tick the other titles too

5. At the top of the list of books, you should see 2 colored buttons, **Delete** and **Deliver**. Of course you want to delete the book so you'll select **Delete** button.

6. Now you have to confirm that you wish to delete. If you went through this all process my accident, you might want to turn back now. But if you're sure you want to delete these guys, Select **Yes, permanently delete**

7. That's not all for confirming, there will be another menu asking you to confirm the action of you permanently delete. You're sure you want to delete so hit **OK**

8. You have to sync your devices to remove the books your library. To sync,

   - Go to the Kindle app. You should see the Kindle icon n your device, tap it

   - At the top right corner of the screen, you should see the 3 dot menu, tap it

   - This should open up the option for you to **Sync and Check for items**. Select this option to remove books

Method 2

From the device

Now this method is applicable if your library is just getting too full and you want to free It a little. As long as you have your device with you then you're ready to roll with this process.

1. Slide over to the home screen on your Kindle. Once you've navigated to the home screen, you can enter the whole Kindle library

if you swipe your finger upwards and downwards

2. After you've gotten to the library, you find have to find the book you wish to remove. You can find it by scrolling down and scanning for the title. But that's pretty hectic. You have the search option, so why don't you use it. It's the magnifying glass at the upper right corner. You'll be able to search or the book by its title

3. After you have found the book you want to remove, press and

hold on the title for a few seconds and then a small menu will show up. From the options that this opens, select the one titled **Remove From Device**. If you tap this option, the book will be deleted from your Kindle device. The book is gone from your device but it's still in the Cloud. If you wish to view it again, you can download it from the cloud

Troubleshooting Kindle problems

Kindle wont charge

Some users of Kindle devices have complained about the problem that they face as they try to charge their device at times. It may be that the Kindle charges very slowly or it doesn't even make an attempt at charging

1. Turn your Kindle off for a start. With the device now turned off, try charging it for a few hours

2. Your Kindle might be totally fine. The problem might originate with the cable. Make sure you use the

cable that came with your device. And if you're using the original cable, check for any sign of the cable wires being exposed or cut

3. If might be that your Kindle has a loose port. Make an attempt of pushing the charger in a bit further.

Kindle just shuts down by itself

You may find that your Kindle just keeps switching of by itself without you press or fiddling with anything. This problem is common among Kindle users. To remedy, you want to try to

1. Charge your battery completely. Make sure you always have enough battery. If your battery is extremely low, it will definitely shut down

2. Try to reset the device by pressing and holding the power button for some time. After Kindle shuts

down, hold the power button again.

3. Maybe your device is overheating. If your device feels hot, remove any protective case and put your Kindle down for a bit.

4. Now the last thing you want to do is factory reset your device

   - Go to **Settings**

   - Then **Device**

   - Choose **Reset to factory Defaults** then **Reset**

Keyboard develops a mind of its own

Some complain that when they are typing with their Kindle, they notice that the keyboard types something totally different, most times gibberish. While the problem might be internal, majority of the causes is the hardware

1. As you use your Kindle, over time it tends to collect dust and oils from your fingers. Seize a microfiber cloth and clean the screen

2. Make sure you're using a screen protector that's compatible with your Kindle. If you are, check that there are no air bubbles underneath the protector. If there is, use a card to draw it out

3. Turn off your device and turn it on again after a few seconds

4. Backup your data and factory reset your device

Kindle won't connect to computer

I might happen that when you try to connect your Kindle to a computer for you transfer files from here to there, it doesn't connect. It might connect at first and then stop or might not even dream of connecting

1. Use the cable that came with your device. Really if there's a matter that requires a cable, use the original cable, your life will be so much easier.

2. Try using a different USB port on the computer

3. Try turning of your Kindle and turning it on a again. Not only your Kindle, shut your computer down and power it on after a while

4. You don't have to cry over transferring with cable, you can just do it over emails

Doesn't give audio

Some have reported that their Kindle doesn't give audio either through the in-built speakers or through headphones

1. Turn up your volume by pressing the Volume up key at the side of your Kindle

2. Try turning of your Kindle and turning it on after a while

3. Try shaking the headphones slightly in the jack and notice if it give off audio through the headphones

4. If the headphones still don't work, try a different one.

Kindle refuses to connect to Wi-Fi

If your Kindle doesn't connect to a Wi-Fi network, you can try the following

1. Remove your Kindle from Airplane mode. To turn airplane mode off, move to **More** then choose **Wireless**

2. To find out if the problem is from your device, use 1 or 2 other devices to connect to the Wi-Fi network. If they don't connect, then the problem is from the network

3. Try turning off your device and switching it on again

4. If nothing works, then you can back up and factory reset your Kindle.

Kindle wont charge

It was mentioned that some users of Kindle devices have complained about the problem that they face as they try to charge their device at times. It may be that the Kindle charges very slowly or it doesn't even make an attempt at charging

- Turn your Kindle off for a start. With the device now turned off, try charging it for a few hours
- Your Kindle might be totally fine. The problem might originate with

the cable. Make sure you use the cable that came with your device. And if you're using the original cable, check for any sign of the cable wires being exposed or cut

➤ If might be that your Kindle has a loose port. Make an attempt of pushing the charger in a bit further.

Haven gone through the whole book, it is believed that you will practice the suggestions and be a pro in managing your Amazon kindle library.

Conclusion

This user guide has delved into important issues surrounding management of kindle library contents. It is believed that you have learned so much from reading the book. You can now create a kindle library easily, borrow books, gift books and share books. The tricks to exploring your kindle library are in your fingertips.

As a reminder, it was mentioned that your kindle fire device can develop issues. The most common issues were highlighted in this text. Let's take the most common of the issues that can bug your Fire tablet, as discussed in this book.

Made in the
USA
Middletown, DE